Chapter 1: Understanding Polarization

The Historical Context of American Polarization

The roots of American polarization can be traced back to the nation's founding, where differing visions for governance and society emerged. The early debates between Federalists and Anti-Federalists highlighted fundamental disagreements about the balance of power between the federal government and the states. These ideological divides laid the groundwork for a political culture characterized by contention and conflict.

The divergence in perspectives on issues such as individual rights, the role of government, and economic policy continued to evolve throughout the 19th century, particularly as the country grappled with the institution of slavery and the question of states' rights.

The Civil War marked a significant turning point in American history, intensifying polarization and setting the stage for a legacy of division that would endure for generations. The war was not merely a conflict over territory but a profound struggle over the moral and social fabric of the nation.

The defeat of the Confederacy did not eradicate the underlying divisions; instead, it entrenched them in the form of Reconstruction policies and the subsequent rise of Jim Crow laws. This period illustrated how historical grievances could foster enduring animosities, contributing to a fractured national identity that would continue to manifest in various forms throughout American history.

The 20th century witnessed the emergence of new ideological battles, particularly during the Cold War era. The ideological clash between capitalism and communism further polarized the American electorate, as domestic policies began to reflect a broader geopolitical struggle. The civil rights movement, while a catalyst for

1

progress, also exposed deep-seated divisions regarding race, equality, and justice.

The backlash against civil rights advancements fueled the rise of conservative movements, which sought to preserve traditional values and resist what they perceived as excessive government intervention in social issues. This period cemented a dichotomy in American politics that would shape the dynamics of future electoral contests.

The late 20th and early 21st centuries brought about the rise of partisan media and the increasing influence of social media platforms, which have exacerbated existing divides. The fragmentation of information sources has created echo chambers where individuals are exposed primarily to viewpoints that reinforce their pre-existing beliefs.

This has contributed to a decline in civil discourse and an increase in polarization, as bipartisan cooperation becomes increasingly rare. The digital age has not only amplified partisan rhetoric but also facilitated the spread of misinformation, further complicating the electorate's ability to engage in informed decision-making.

As America stands at a crossroads, understanding the historical context of polarization is crucial for navigating its future. The interplay of ideology, identity, and technology has created a complex landscape that demands a renewed commitment to dialogue and collaboration. The specter of a new civil war, while often sensationalized, underscores the urgency of addressing the underlying issues that divide the nation.

By reflecting on the lessons of history, the electorate can work towards fostering a more inclusive and cohesive democracy, ensuring that the fractures of the past do not dictate the future trajectory of the American political landscape.

The Role of Media in Dividing Opinions

The role of media in shaping public opinion has evolved dramatically over the past few decades, particularly with the rise of digital platforms. Traditional media outlets, once seen as gatekeepers of information, have been joined by a plethora of online sources that cater to specific ideologies and preferences.

This shift has created an environment where individuals can easily find news that aligns with their beliefs, leading to the reinforcement of existing opinions rather than fostering a culture of open dialogue. As a result, the media landscape has become a battleground for competing narratives, contributing to the polarization of the electorate.

Social media platforms, in particular, have exacerbated divisions by creating echo chambers where like-minded individuals congregate. Algorithms designed to maximize engagement often promote sensational content that elicits strong emotional reactions. This amplification of extreme viewpoints can distort public discourse, making it more difficult for people to engage with differing perspectives.

As users become increasingly isolated in their ideological bubbles, the potential for misunderstanding and hostility toward opposing views grows, further entrenching societal divisions.

Moreover, the increasing reliance on partisan news sources has led to the fragmentation of the media landscape. Audiences are now more likely to consume information that confirms their biases, as partisan outlets tend to frame stories in ways that resonate with their viewers' pre-existing beliefs. This trend not only undermines the objectivity of reporting but also diminishes the public's ability to critically evaluate information.

When significant portions of the electorate rely on skewed narratives, the potential for informed consensus diminishes, leaving the nation at risk of deeper divisions.

The implications of this media-driven polarization extend beyond individual opinions; they have profound effects on the democratic process itself. As citizens become more entrenched in their viewpoints, the willingness to compromise diminishes, making it increasingly challenging to achieve bipartisan cooperation on critical issues.

This lack of collaboration can lead to legislative gridlock and exacerbate feelings of disenfranchisement among those who feel their concerns are not being addressed. In this context, the media's role in dividing opinions becomes a significant factor in the overall health of American democracy.

Addressing this polarization requires a concerted effort to promote media literacy and encourage critical consumption of information. Citizens must be equipped with the tools to navigate the complex media landscape, distinguishing between credible sources and those that prioritize sensationalism over factual reporting.

By fostering a culture of open dialogue and encouraging exposure to diverse viewpoints, the electorate can begin to bridge the divides that threaten the stability of American democracy. In doing so, the media can transition from a source of division to a catalyst for understanding, ultimately contributing to a more unified and resilient society.

Social Media and the Echo Chamber Effect

Social media has become a dominant force in shaping public discourse, particularly in the context of American democracy. Its ability to connect individuals across vast distances allows for the rapid dissemination of information, but this same power raises critical concerns about the echo chamber effect.

This phenomenon occurs when individuals are exposed primarily to information and opinions that reinforce their preexisting beliefs, leading to increased polarization and a diminished capacity for constructive dialogue. As the United States grapples with deepening divisions, understanding the echo chamber effect is essential for addressing the challenges facing the democratic process.

The algorithms governing social media platforms are designed to maximize user engagement by promoting content that aligns with users' interests. This leads to the creation of curated information environments where dissenting viewpoints are marginalized or excluded altogether.

As users interact primarily with like-minded individuals and content, they become entrenched in their perspectives, often viewing opposing views as not only incorrect but also as a threat to their identity and values. This narrowing of discourse hampers the potential for compromise, making it increasingly difficult for citizens to engage in meaningful discussions about critical issues affecting the nation.

Moreover, the echo chamber effect contributes to the spread of misinformation and conspiracy theories, which can further exacerbate societal divisions. When individuals are isolated within their ideological bubbles, they are more susceptible to accepting false narratives that align with their beliefs. This not only distorts public understanding of key issues but also fosters an environment where trust in established institutions erodes.

As citizens become more reliant on social media as a primary source of news and information, the potential for misinformation to influence political opinions and behaviors grows, posing a significant threat to the integrity of democratic processes.

The implications of the echo chamber effect extend beyond individual beliefs, as they influence collective political behavior. Polarization fueled by social media can manifest in various ways, including increased hostility towards political opponents, heightened partisanship, and a decline in civic engagement. This dynamic can complicate governance, as elected officials may cater to their polarized bases rather than seeking common ground.

The consequences are far-reaching, potentially leading to legislative gridlock and a diminished capacity for the government to respond effectively to pressing national issues.

Addressing the challenges posed by social media and the echo chamber effect requires a multifaceted approach. Efforts must be made to promote media literacy among the electorate, encouraging critical evaluation of information sources and fostering a willingness to engage with diverse perspectives.

Additionally, social media platforms must take responsibility for their role in facilitating polarization, implementing algorithms that prioritize exposure to a broader range of viewpoints. Ultimately, restoring a healthy democratic discourse and bridging the growing divide will depend on the collective commitment to engage constructively, challenge our assumptions, and seek common ground in an increasingly fragmented information landscape.

Chapter 2: The Roots of Division

Economic Disparities and Class Divide

Economic disparities in the United States have reached unprecedented levels, contributing to a growing class divide that poses significant challenges to the fabric of American democracy. The widening gap between the wealthy and the poor undermines the principle of equal opportunity, which is foundational to democratic ideals. As a result, the affluent continue to accumulate resources and influence, while many Americans struggle to meet basic needs.

This economic stratification not only affects individual lives but also has broader implications for civic engagement and political participation.

The effects of economic inequality extend beyond mere financial hardship. Communities that experience higher levels of poverty often face systemic barriers that further entrench their disadvantages. Access to quality education, healthcare, and job opportunities becomes limited, perpetuating a cycle of disadvantage that is difficult to escape.

As a consequence, individuals from lower socioeconomic backgrounds may feel disenfranchised and disconnected from the political process, fostering a sense of alienation and disillusionment with democratic institutions. This disconnection can lead to lower voter turnout and reduced civic participation, exacerbating the divide between different social classes.

Moreover, economic disparities fuel polarization among the electorate. As individuals align themselves with groups that reflect their economic interests, political affiliations can become increasingly defined by class. This alignment often results in a lack of empathy and understanding between different socioeconomic groups, deepening societal divisions.

Political discourse becomes dominated by the concerns of the affluent, often neglecting the pressing issues faced by lower-income populations. Consequently, policy decisions may reflect the priorities of the wealthy, further widening the gap and leading to a perception that democracy favors the elite.

The intersection of class and economic inequality also has ramifications for social mobility. Many Americans believe in the idea of the "American Dream," yet the reality is that upward mobility has stagnated for a significant portion of the population. High levels of student debt, rising housing costs, and stagnant wages have made it increasingly difficult for individuals to improve their socioeconomic status.

This stagnation not only impacts personal aspirations but also challenges the narrative of meritocracy that is central to American identity. As the dream becomes less attainable, frustration and resentment can fester, potentially igniting social unrest.

Addressing economic disparities and the class divide is essential for the health of American democracy. Creating inclusive economic policies that promote equitable growth is crucial for rebuilding trust in democratic institutions. Initiatives that focus on improving access to education, healthcare, and economic opportunities for all citizens can help bridge the divide and foster a more engaged electorate.

As the nation grapples with its polarized future, recognizing and addressing the complexities of economic disparities will be vital in ensuring that democracy serves the interests of all Americans, rather than a privileged few.

Racial and Ethnic Tensions

Racial and ethnic tensions in the United States have deep historical roots, often manifesting as significant barriers to social cohesion and democratic progress. These tensions are exacerbated by socio-economic disparities, systemic discrimination, and a political landscape that frequently exploits divisions for electoral gain.

As the nation grapples with its identity amidst demographic changes, the ramifications of these tensions become increasingly pronounced, raising critical questions about the future of American democracy and its capacity to navigate profound divisions without descending into conflict.

The demographic shifts in the U.S. are significant, with projections indicating that by 2045, the nation will become "minority-majority," where no single racial or ethnic group holds a majority. This transformation, while potentially enriching the fabric of American society, also poses challenges.

Many individuals may feel threatened by the prospect of losing cultural dominance or economic opportunities, prompting a defensive response that often manifests as hostility toward minority groups. Such sentiments can fuel political polarization, where parties and candidates exploit fears and anxieties to galvanize support, further entrenching divisions and complicating efforts toward unity.

Political discourse surrounding race and ethnicity has become increasingly charged, often reflecting broader societal anxieties about identity and belonging. The rhetoric employed by political leaders can either exacerbate tensions or foster a climate of understanding and collaboration.

Unfortunately, instances of dog-whistle politics and inflammatory rhetoric have become commonplace, creating an environment where dialogue about race is fraught with fear and misunderstanding. This climate undermines the foundational principles of democracy, where open discourse and mutual respect should prevail, and instead cultivates an atmosphere ripe for conflict.

Moreover, the impact of social media and digital communication has intensified racial and ethnic tensions, allowing for the rapid spread of misinformation and divisive narratives. Online platforms often serve as echo chambers, amplifying extreme viewpoints and minimizing opportunities for constructive engagement.

The algorithms that govern these platforms tend to prioritize sensational content, which can deepen divisions and polarize communities. As citizens increasingly turn to these digital spaces for news and information, the potential for misunderstanding and hostility grows, raising concerns about the capacity for democratic dialogue in such an environment.

Addressing racial and ethnic tensions is imperative for the survival of American democracy. It requires a multifaceted approach that includes educational initiatives aimed at fostering understanding, policy reforms that address systemic inequities, and a commitment from political leaders to rise above divisive rhetoric.

Building a more inclusive democracy hinges on the ability to engage in honest conversations about race and ethnicity, recognizing the shared humanity that transcends our differences. Only by confronting these challenges head-on can the nation hope to navigate its polarized future without succumbing to the specter of civil strife.

Ideological Extremism

Ideological extremism has emerged as a significant threat to American democracy, manifesting through fervent beliefs that reject compromise and dialogue. This phenomenon is marked by an unwavering commitment to a particular set of ideas, often at the expense of democratic principles such as tolerance, pluralism, and respect for opposing viewpoints.

The rise of social media platforms has exacerbated this issue, allowing extremist ideologies to proliferate and gain traction among disaffected populations. As citizens increasingly consume news and information that aligns with their pre-existing beliefs, the ability to engage in constructive conversation diminishes, leading to a fragmented society.

The consequences of ideological extremism are evident in the growing political polarization that characterizes contemporary America. This polarization is not merely a matter of differing opinions but has evolved into a deep-seated animosity between groups that perceive each other as existential threats. As political discourse deteriorates, the potential for violence escalates.

Incidents of politically motivated violence, often fueled by extremist rhetoric, highlight the alarming reality that some individuals are willing to resort to force to achieve their objectives. This trend poses a direct challenge to the foundational tenets of democracy, which rely on peaceful conflict resolution and respect for the rule of law.

Moreover, ideological extremism has infiltrated major political institutions, complicating the governance process. Elected officials and party leaders often find themselves beholden to the radical elements within their base, leading to a reluctance to engage in bipartisan collaboration. This dynamic stifles effective policymaking and reinforces the idea that compromise is a sign of weakness.

The inability to navigate the complexities of governance in a pluralistic society not only undermines public trust in democratic institutions but also fosters an environment where extremist factions can flourish, further entrenching the divide.

The implications of these developments extend beyond the political realm, affecting social cohesion and community resilience. As individuals retreat into ideological silos, the shared understanding necessary for a functional democracy erodes. Communities become polarized, with individuals viewing their neighbors as adversaries rather than fellow citizens.

This breakdown in social fabric can hinder collective action on pressing issues, such as climate change, economic inequality, and public health, which require collaborative solutions. The challenge lies in rekindling the spirit of civic engagement and fostering environments where diverse perspectives can coexist and contribute to the common good.

Addressing ideological extremism requires a multifaceted approach that emphasizes education, dialogue, and community-building. Initiatives aimed at promoting critical thinking and media literacy can empower citizens to critically assess information and engage with opposing viewpoints. Furthermore, fostering spaces for open and respectful dialogue can help bridge divides and restore a sense of shared identity.

Ultimately, the future of American democracy hinges on the electorate's ability to confront ideological extremism with resilience and commitment to the core values that underpin democratic governance. Only through collective efforts can the nation hope to navigate the challenges posed by polarization and move toward a more inclusive and robust democratic future.

Chapter 3: The Political Landscape

The Rise of Partisan Politics

The rise of partisan politics in the United States has fundamentally altered the landscape of American democracy. Historically, political factions have existed, but the current climate is marked by an unprecedented level of polarization that permeates both political institutions and the general electorate.

This trend can be traced back to various societal changes, including the realignment of political parties, the increasing influence of social media, and the growing importance of identity politics. As these factors intertwine, they contribute to a divisive atmosphere that challenges the foundational principles of democratic governance.

One significant factor in the rise of partisan politics is the realignment of the political parties themselves. Over the past few decades, the Republican and Democratic parties have undergone substantial transformations, with shifts in their platforms and voter bases. These changes have often been driven by demographic shifts and evolving public sentiments, resulting in a more homogenous and ideologically rigid party structure.

This realignment has fostered an environment where compromise becomes increasingly rare, as party loyalty often supersedes collaborative governance. The result is a political arena marked by hostility and an unwillingness to engage with opposing viewpoints.

The advent of social media has further exacerbated partisan divides, transforming the way information is disseminated and consumed. Platforms such as Twitter and Facebook have become battlegrounds for ideological conflicts, where echo chambers amplify partisan rhetoric and reinforce existing beliefs.

The algorithms that govern these platforms often prioritize sensational content, leading to the spread of misinformation and the entrenchment of extreme viewpoints. This digital landscape not only influences individual perceptions but also shapes public discourse, contributing to a climate where civil debate is increasingly overshadowed by vitriol.

Identity politics has emerged as another pivotal force in the rise of partisan politics. The emphasis on race, gender, and other aspects of identity has led to a more fragmented political landscape, where individuals align themselves with parties based on shared experiences rather than broader ideological principles. While this focus can empower marginalized voices, it can also create divisions that hinder collective action on critical issues.

As voters gravitate toward parties that affirm their identities, the potential for bipartisan cooperation diminishes, further entrenching the polarization that characterizes contemporary American politics.

Looking ahead, the implications of rising partisan politics are profound. The potential for a new civil war, while often sensationalized, is not unfounded when considering the extent of division within the electorate. As citizens increasingly view political opponents as existential threats, the foundation of democratic engagement erodes.

For American democracy to endure, it is imperative to seek avenues for dialogue and understanding, transcending the current polarized environment. Without concerted efforts to bridge these divides, the future of American governance remains precarious, threatening the very principles upon which the nation was founded.

The Impact of Gerrymandering

Gerrymandering, the manipulation of electoral district boundaries for partisan advantage, poses a significant threat to the integrity of American democracy. This practice allows political parties to entrench their power by drawing districts that favor their candidates, thereby undermining the principle of fair representation.

As legislators prioritize self-preservation over the needs of their constituents, voter disenfranchisement and political polarization intensify, leading to a cycle of division that jeopardizes the foundational ideals of democratic governance.

The consequences of gerrymandering extend beyond skewed electoral outcomes; they foster an environment where compromise becomes increasingly rare. When districts are designed to ensure victories for one party, elected officials may cater exclusively to their base, ignoring the broader electorate's concerns.

This lack of accountability diminishes the incentive for bipartisanship and constructive dialogue, further entrenching divisions within the political landscape. As a result, citizens may feel disillusioned and alienated from the political process, believing their voices are irrelevant in a system that seems rigged against them.

Moreover, gerrymandering contributes to the erosion of trust in democratic institutions. As voters witness the manipulation of district lines, they may begin to question the legitimacy of elections and the motives of their representatives. This skepticism can lead to decreased voter turnout and engagement, creating a vicious cycle where disillusionment breeds apathy.

When citizens feel that their participation in democracy is futile, the very fabric of civil society begins to fray, raising concerns about the stability of the political system and the potential for unrest.

The implications of gerrymandering are particularly pronounced in an era characterized by heightened political polarization. As parties become more entrenched in their ideological positions, the ability to engage across the aisle diminishes, exacerbating tensions within society.

The stark divisions fostered by gerrymandered districts can create echo chambers, where individuals are insulated from differing viewpoints, reinforcing extreme beliefs and diminishing the possibility of consensus. This environment raises concerns about the potential for civil discord, as communities become more fragmented and distrustful of one another.

Ultimately, addressing the impact of gerrymandering is essential for safeguarding the future of American democracy. Reform efforts, such as independent redistricting commissions and enhanced transparency in the redistricting process, aim to restore fairness and accountability to electoral systems.

By prioritizing the interests of the electorate over partisan gain, these initiatives can help rebuild trust in democratic institutions and foster a more inclusive political environment. As the nation grapples with questions of unity and division, confronting the challenges posed by gerrymandering is a crucial step in ensuring a resilient and equitable democracy for future generations.

The Role of Political Parties in Polarization

Political parties play a pivotal role in shaping the landscape of American democracy, particularly in the context of increasing polarization. Over the last few decades, the ideological divide between the two major parties, Democrats and Republicans, has widened significantly. This polarization is not merely a reflection of differing policy preferences but also a deep-seated cultural and social schism.

As parties align more closely with specific demographic groups, they foster an environment where compromise becomes increasingly rare, and political identities become entrenched. This dynamic raises critical questions about the future of governance and unity in the United States.

The mechanisms through which political parties contribute to polarization are multifaceted. Primarily, parties serve as gatekeepers of political discourse, controlling the narratives that dominate public debate. By framing issues in a way that highlights differences rather than commonalities, parties can exacerbate divisions among the electorate.

Furthermore, the rise of partisan media has amplified this effect, as individuals increasingly consume information that reinforces their existing beliefs. This media environment, often characterized by echo chambers, reduces exposure to alternative viewpoints, solidifying partisan identities and making it more challenging for individuals to engage in constructive dialogue across the aisle.

Moreover, the strategic choices made by political parties in their pursuit of electoral success have further intensified polarization. The practice of gerrymandering, for instance, has created safe districts where incumbents face little competition from opposing parties. This allows elected officials to cater to their base rather than seeking bipartisan support, further entrenching ideological extremes.

Additionally, the increasing reliance on negative campaigning and attack ads diminishes the focus on policy discussion, instead fostering animosity towards the opposing party. These tactics contribute to a political culture where loyalty to party often overshadows allegiance to democratic principles.

The implications of this polarization extend beyond the political realm, affecting social cohesion and community relations. As party affiliation becomes synonymous with personal identity, social interactions increasingly gravitate towards like-minded individuals, leading to the fragmentation of society.

This phenomenon can create an atmosphere of mistrust and hostility towards those who hold differing views, undermining the foundational tenets of democratic engagement. Such a societal divide poses significant challenges to collective problem-solving and governance, raising concerns about the viability of democratic institutions in an increasingly polarized environment.

Addressing the role of political parties in polarization requires a concerted effort from both leaders and the electorate. Initiatives aimed at fostering bipartisanship and encouraging civil discourse are essential in bridging divides. Electorate engagement in local politics, coupled with support for reforms that promote fair representation and accountability, can help mitigate the negative effects of polarization.

As the United States navigates its polarized future, a renewed commitment to democratic values and an understanding of the complexities surrounding political parties will be crucial in averting an increasingly divided society.

Chapter 4: Public Opinion and Civil Discourse

Changing Attitudes Toward Governance

In recent years, the American electorate has witnessed a profound transformation in attitudes toward governance, driven by a combination of social, economic, and technological factors. This shift reflects a growing disillusionment with traditional political institutions and an increasing demand for transparency and accountability.

Citizens are no longer content to accept the status quo; instead, they actively seek to influence policy decisions and hold elected officials responsible for their actions. This change has significant implications for the future of American democracy, as it challenges long-standing norms and fosters an environment where political engagement is both encouraged and expected.

Moreover, the rise of social media has played a crucial role in reshaping public discourse around governance. Platforms such as Twitter and Facebook have democratized information dissemination, allowing individuals to voice their opinions, organize movements, and mobilize support for various causes. This newfound accessibility to information has empowered citizens, but it has also contributed to the polarization of public opinion.

As people increasingly curate their news sources to align with their beliefs, the potential for constructive dialogue diminishes, leading to an environment where compromise becomes increasingly elusive.

In addition to technological influences, the changing demographics of the United States have also impacted attitudes toward governance. A younger, more diverse electorate is demanding policies that reflect their values and priorities. Issues such as climate change, social justice, and economic inequality resonate deeply with this demographic, driving a desire for governance that is not only responsive but proactive.

As these voices gain prominence, traditional political alliances may shift, forcing established parties to adapt to the evolving landscape or risk alienating a significant portion of the electorate.

The implications of these changing attitudes extend beyond mere electoral outcomes; they raise critical questions about the future of American democratic institutions. As citizens become more engaged and outspoken, the pressure on lawmakers to address systemic issues intensifies. This dynamic can lead to a more vibrant democracy, where diverse perspectives are represented, and accountability is prioritized.

However, it also poses risks, as heightened demands for immediate action may result in frustration and disillusionment if change is not perceived as swift or sufficient.

Ultimately, navigating this landscape of changing attitudes toward governance will require a concerted effort from all stakeholders in American democracy. Elected officials must cultivate an environment of trust and openness, recognizing that the electorate's engagement is a vital component of a healthy democracy. Meanwhile, citizens must remain committed to constructive dialogue and collaboration, striving to bridge divides rather than deepen them.

As America faces the prospect of a polarized future, the choices made today will shape the trajectory of governance and the resilience of democracy for generations to come.

The Decline of Bipartisan Cooperation

The decline of bipartisan cooperation in American politics has significantly altered the landscape of governance, leading to increased polarization and a growing rift among the electorate. This shift is not merely a recent development but has been years in the making, influenced by various social, economic, and technological factors.

As political parties have become more ideologically homogenous, the willingness to collaborate across the aisle has diminished. This erosion of cooperation is evident in the legislative gridlock that has become a hallmark of contemporary governance, where compromise is often seen as capitulation rather than a necessary component of democratic function.

One of the primary drivers of this decline is the changing nature of political identity. Voters increasingly align themselves with parties that reflect their values and beliefs, leading to an environment where loyalty to party ideology supersedes the pursuit of common ground. This identity-driven politics fosters an adversarial stance, where opposing parties are viewed not just as rivals but as threats to one's own way of life.

Such a mindset creates an echo chamber effect, wherein individuals are less likely to engage with differing viewpoints, exacerbating divisions within the electorate and diminishing the prospect for bipartisan dialogue.

Moreover, the role of media and technology cannot be understated in this dynamic. The rise of partisan news outlets and social media platforms has contributed to the fragmentation of information sources, allowing individuals to curate their news consumption in ways that reinforce their existing beliefs.

This phenomenon not only isolates voters from opposing perspectives but also cultivates an environment where misinformation can thrive. As citizens become more entrenched in their views, the potential for constructive discourse diminishes, further entrenching the divide between political parties.

Institutional factors also play a critical role in the decline of bipartisan cooperation. The design of the political system, including gerrymandering and the increasing frequency of primary elections, often favors candidates who cater to the extremes of their party. This electoral strategy discourages moderation and incentivizes politicians to adopt more polarized positions, as primary voters tend to be more ideologically driven than the general electorate.

Consequently, elected officials are less likely to seek bipartisan solutions, fearing backlash from their own party constituents for engaging with the opposition.

As the United States faces these challenges, the implications for democracy are profound. The decline of bipartisan cooperation not only stifles effective governance but also raises concerns about the stability of the political system itself. If compromise and collaboration continue to diminish, the risk of further polarization escalates, potentially leading to a more fragmented society.

In this context, it becomes essential for the electorate to critically assess the value of cooperation and seek pathways to restore a sense of unity in governance, lest the nation drift further toward a state of political unrest and division reminiscent of more tumultuous periods in American history.

The Erosion of Trust in Institutions

The erosion of trust in institutions has become a defining characteristic of contemporary American society, reflecting a profound shift in the relationship between citizens and the structures that govern them. Over the past few decades, various institutions, including government, media, and even academia, have faced increasing skepticism from the public. This decline in trust is not merely a fleeting concern; it poses a significant threat to the fabric of democracy itself.

When citizens no longer believe in the legitimacy or efficacy of their institutions, the potential for polarization and conflict grows, raising questions about the stability of democratic governance in the United States.

A multitude of factors has contributed to this erosion of trust. Political polarization has intensified, leading to a scenario where individuals align their beliefs closely with partisan identities. As political discourse becomes more hostile and divisive, adherence to shared facts and common narratives diminishes.

This fragmentation has been exacerbated by the rise of social media platforms, which often amplify misinformation and create echo chambers that reinforce existing biases. Consequently, institutions that once served as neutral arbiters of information and governance are now viewed through the lens of partisanship, further undermining their credibility.

The implications of diminished trust extend beyond mere perception; they affect public policy and civic engagement. When citizens feel disconnected from their institutions, participation in democratic processes—such as voting, community organizing, and public discourse—declines. The disengagement of the electorate not only weakens the democratic process but also gives rise to apathy and cynicism.

In this environment, radical ideologies can flourish, as marginalized groups may seek alternative means of influence outside traditional democratic channels. The potential for unrest increases when segments of the population perceive that their voices are not heard or valued within the existing institutional framework.

Moreover, the erosion of trust can lead to a vicious cycle that further entrenches divisions within society. As institutions fail to respond effectively to the needs and concerns of the populace, disillusionment grows, prompting calls for radical reforms or even the complete dismantling of established systems. This sentiment can manifest in movements that challenge the status quo, fostering an environment ripe for conflict and potential violence.

The prospect of a new civil war, while often sensationalized, is not entirely unfounded; it reflects the underlying fractures within American society that could emerge if trust continues to deteriorate.

Restoring trust in institutions is a complex challenge that requires concerted efforts across various sectors of society. It demands a commitment to transparency, accountability, and genuine engagement from both leaders and citizens. As the electorate grapples with its role in shaping the future of American democracy, it is crucial to recognize the importance of rebuilding the foundations of trust.

Only through collaborative efforts can the nation hope to bridge the existing divides and foster a more inclusive, resilient democratic system capable of withstanding the pressures of polarization and discontent.

Chapter 5: The Threat of Authoritarianism

Signs of Authoritarian Tendencies

The signs of authoritarian tendencies in a democratic society can manifest in various forms, often subtly at first, before escalating into more overt actions. One significant indicator is the erosion of institutional checks and balances. When political leaders begin to undermine the independence of the judiciary, manipulate electoral processes, or weaken legislative oversight, it sets a dangerous precedent.

Such actions signal a departure from democratic principles, as they concentrate power in the hands of a few and diminish the role of accountability. The manipulation of institutions can foster a culture where dissent is stifled, and the rule of law becomes secondary to the interests of those in power.

Another critical sign is the use of rhetoric that seeks to delegitimize opposition. Authoritarian leaders often employ language that frames dissenters as enemies of the state or as threats to national security. This tactic not only polarizes the electorate but also creates an environment where political violence can flourish. When political discourse shifts from debate to denigration, it undermines the core democratic values of tolerance and pluralism.

In such an atmosphere, citizens may feel compelled to choose sides, leading to further division and a potential breakdown of civil discourse.

The rise of populist movements can also indicate authoritarian tendencies, especially when they promote a singular narrative that dismisses complex societal issues. Populism often thrives on the idea of a corrupt elite versus a virtuous common people, which can lead to scapegoating and the marginalization of minority groups. This dynamic can erode social cohesion and foster an "us versus them" mentality, making it easier for authoritarian figures to gain support.

By simplifying complex problems and offering simplistic solutions, populist leaders can manipulate public sentiment, steering the electorate away from democratic ideals and towards authoritarian governance.

Additionally, the manipulation of media and the spread of misinformation are potent indicators of authoritarianism. Control over information allows leaders to shape public perception and suppress dissenting viewpoints. When state-sponsored narratives dominate the media landscape, citizens are deprived of the diverse perspectives necessary for informed decision-making.

The proliferation of disinformation further complicates the landscape, as it breeds distrust in legitimate sources of information. This can result in an electorate that is ill-equipped to critically engage with political issues, ultimately paving the way for authoritarian practices to take root.

Lastly, the normalization of political violence poses a grave threat to democracy. When political disagreements escalate into violence, it not only undermines the principles of democratic engagement but also instills fear within the populace. The acceptance of intimidation tactics, whether through protests or threats against political opponents, erodes the foundational belief in resolving disputes through dialogue and compromise.

As society becomes desensitized to such behavior, the potential for civil conflict increases, raising the specter of a fractured nation. Recognizing these signs is crucial for the electorate, as vigilance and active engagement are essential to safeguarding democracy against the encroachment of authoritarianism.

Historical Parallels with Past Regimes

Historical parallels with past regimes provide a valuable lens through which to analyze the current state of American democracy, particularly amidst rising polarization. As the U.S. grapples with divisions reminiscent of earlier conflicts, such as the Civil War and the McCarthy era, understanding these historical contexts can illuminate the challenges facing the electorate today.

These periods were marked by intense ideological battles, social upheaval, and questions of national identity, all of which resonate in today's political climate.

The Civil War era serves as a stark reminder of the consequences of deep-seated divisions. The schism between the North and South was not solely about slavery but also about differing visions of governance, state rights, and societal organization. Today, we witness a similar fracturing along ideological lines, where debates over issues such as immigration, healthcare, and climate change reflect broader struggles over American identity and values.

This historical parallel raises critical questions about the potential for conflict and the means by which society can navigate such divisions without resorting to violence or civil strife.

Another significant period to consider is the McCarthy era of the 1950s, characterized by widespread fear, suspicion, and the politicization of identity. The Red Scare fostered an environment where dissent was often equated with disloyalty, leading to the persecution of individuals based on their beliefs or associations. In contemporary America, we see echoes of this dynamic through the increasing vilification of opposing political ideologies.

The rise of hyperpartisanship and the willingness to label dissenting voices as threats to national security or societal cohesion echo the tactics employed during McCarthyism, raising concerns about the implications for free speech and democratic discourse.

Furthermore, the historical context of civil rights movements illustrates the ongoing struggle for equity and justice within the framework of American democracy. The fight against systemic racism and inequality has been a persistent theme throughout U.S. history, often met with resistance and backlash from those who perceive these movements as threats to their status.

The current discourse surrounding issues of racial justice, police reform, and social equity reflects a similar tension. As the electorate navigates these complex issues, it is essential to recognize the historical struggles that have shaped contemporary debates and the need for inclusive dialogue to foster understanding and progress.

In examining these historical parallels, it becomes clear that the lessons learned from past regimes can inform our approach to the present challenges. The importance of fostering inclusive political dialogue, protecting civil liberties, and promoting social cohesion cannot be overstated. As the U.S.

electorate stands at a crossroads, the capacity to draw from history can provide crucial insights into preventing the escalation of polarization into outright conflict. By understanding the roots of division and the pathways to reconciliation, Americans can work towards a more unified and resilient democratic future.

The Role of Leadership in a Democratic Society

Leadership in a democratic society plays a pivotal role in shaping the political landscape and fostering a culture of civic engagement. Effective leaders are essential for bridging divides, promoting dialogue, and ensuring that diverse voices are heard in the decision-making process. In the context of a polarized America, the influence of leadership becomes even more pronounced as it can either exacerbate tensions or facilitate understanding.

Leaders must remain committed to the foundational principles of democracy, prioritizing collaboration over confrontation, and working to unite constituents around shared values and goals.

One of the most significant responsibilities of leaders in a democratic society is to model ethical behavior and integrity. Leaders set the tone for political discourse and public engagement, and their actions can inspire or demoralize the electorate. When leaders prioritize honesty, transparency, and accountability, they foster trust within the community.

This trust is essential for a healthy democracy, as it encourages citizens to participate in the political process and hold their representatives accountable. Conversely, leaders who engage in divisive rhetoric or unethical practices can undermine democratic norms and alienate segments of the population, exacerbating polarization.

In navigating the complexities of a polarized society, leaders must also prioritize inclusivity. A successful democracy relies on the active participation of its citizens, which necessitates that all voices are represented and valued. Leaders who actively seek to engage marginalized communities and promote diverse perspectives contribute to a more robust democratic process.

By creating avenues for dialogue and encouraging participation from all demographics, leaders can help mitigate feelings of disenfranchisement and foster a sense of belonging among constituents. This inclusivity not only enriches the democratic experience but also strengthens societal cohesion.

Moreover, the role of leadership extends beyond the political arena; leaders must also cultivate an informed and engaged electorate. In an era characterized by misinformation and polarized media, it is crucial for leaders to prioritize education and critical thinking within their constituencies.

By promoting civic education initiatives and encouraging media literacy, leaders can empower citizens to make informed decisions and engage in constructive debates. Leaders who prioritize these efforts contribute to a more resilient democracy, equipping citizens with the tools necessary to navigate complex political landscapes and make sense of differing viewpoints.

Ultimately, the effectiveness of leadership in a democratic society is contingent upon a commitment to the principles of democracy itself. As the nation grapples with increasing polarization and the specter of civil conflict, leaders must rise to the occasion, demonstrating courage, empathy, and a dedication to the common good.

By fostering collaboration, promoting inclusivity, and encouraging civic engagement, leaders can play a crucial role in steering America toward a more unified and resilient democratic future. The choices made by leaders today will not only impact the present political climate but also shape the course of American democracy for generations to come.

Chapter 6: The Future of Civic Engagement

The Importance of Grassroots Movements

Grassroots movements play a pivotal role in shaping the landscape of American democracy, especially in an era marked by increasing polarization. These movements arise organically from the community level, driven by individuals who share common concerns and aspirations.

Unlike top-down approaches, grassroots efforts empower citizens to engage directly in the democratic process, fostering a sense of ownership and agency among the electorate. As the nation grapples with deep ideological divides, understanding the importance of grassroots movements becomes essential for navigating the complexities of contemporary democracy.

One of the primary strengths of grassroots movements lies in their ability to mobilize diverse groups around shared goals. By harnessing the collective power of individuals, these movements can amplify voices that might otherwise go unheard. This inclusivity is particularly vital in a polarized environment where mainstream narratives often marginalize certain perspectives.

Grassroots initiatives create spaces for dialogue and collaboration, enabling constituents to come together across differences and advocate for policies that reflect their collective interests. In doing so, they not only enhance civic engagement but also contribute to a more representative democratic process.

Moreover, grassroots movements serve as a form of resistance against entrenched power structures. As citizens become disillusioned with traditional political institutions, they often look to grassroots organizing as a means of effecting change. These movements challenge the status quo by highlighting issues that may be neglected by established political parties or leaders.

By focusing on local concerns—be it social justice, environmental protection, or economic inequality—grassroots organizers can shift the narrative and push for reforms that resonate with the electorate. This dynamic is crucial in preventing the erosion of democratic principles and ensuring that the voices of ordinary Americans are not drowned out by the interests of the powerful.

The impact of grassroots movements extends beyond immediate policy changes; they also play a critical role in shaping the future of political engagement in the United States. As younger generations become increasingly involved in activism, grassroots movements are evolving in response to their needs and aspirations.

This generational shift is fostering innovative strategies for mobilization, such as the use of social media and digital platforms, which can reach wider audiences and inspire collective action. The ability to adapt to changing communication landscapes enhances the relevance and efficacy of grassroots efforts, positioning them as key players in the ongoing struggle for a more democratic society.

In conclusion, the significance of grassroots movements in the context of America's polarized future cannot be overstated. These movements not only empower individuals to reclaim their agency within the democratic process but also challenge systemic injustices and promote inclusivity. As the electorate faces the potential for further division, it is imperative to recognize and support the work being done at the grassroots level.

By fostering collaboration and encouraging active participation, these movements can help bridge divides and reinforce the foundational principles of democracy, ultimately steering the nation away from the brink of a new civil war toward a more unified and equitable future.

Engaging the Youth in Democracy

Engaging the youth in democracy is not merely an option; it is an imperative for the health of our political system. As the demographic landscape of America evolves, the voices and perspectives of younger generations become increasingly crucial in shaping the future of democracy. With rising polarization, it is essential to cultivate a sense of civic responsibility among young people, encouraging them to actively participate in the democratic process.

This engagement can take many forms, from voting to community organizing, and is vital in countering the divisive narratives that threaten the fabric of our society.

One of the most effective ways to engage youth is through education that emphasizes critical thinking and civic literacy. Schools and universities must prioritize curricula that not only teach the mechanics of government but also encourage students to understand the importance of their participation in democracy. This includes discussions on current events, the impact of policy decisions, and the role of grassroots movements.

By fostering an environment where young people can explore their values and beliefs, we empower them to become informed citizens who are equipped to challenge polarization and advocate for their communities.

In addition to educational initiatives, leveraging technology and social media can play a transformative role in engaging young people. Digital platforms provide unique opportunities for outreach and mobilization, allowing for more dynamic forms of political engagement.

Campaigns that use social media to connect with youth can break down barriers to participation, making it easier for young voters to access information, share their opinions, and organize around issues they care about. This technological engagement can also help to cultivate a sense of community among young activists, fostering collaboration across diverse backgrounds and ideologies.

Furthermore, it is crucial to create inclusive spaces where young voices are not just heard but actively sought out in political discussions. This can be achieved through initiatives that encourage young people to participate in local governance, such as youth councils or town hall meetings that prioritize their input.

By creating a culture that values youth perspectives, we not only strengthen the democratic process but also instill a sense of ownership and responsibility among young citizens. This involvement can serve as a counterweight to the alienation many feel in today's political landscape, helping to bridge the divide between generations.

Ultimately, engaging the youth in democracy is essential for addressing the challenges we face as a nation. By investing in education, utilizing technology, and creating inclusive platforms for participation, we can cultivate a politically active youth that is committed to a more equitable and just society.

As America navigates its polarized future, empowering the next generation of leaders and citizens will be crucial in preventing further division and fostering a renewed commitment to democratic ideals. The future of American democracy depends on the active and informed participation of its youth, ensuring that they play a pivotal role in shaping the nation's path forward.

Revitalizing Community Involvement

Revitalizing community involvement is critical to strengthening the fabric of American democracy, particularly in an era characterized by polarization and division. A vibrant, engaged citizenry is essential for the functioning of a healthy democracy. Citizens who actively participate in their communities help foster a sense of belonging and shared purpose.

This engagement not only enhances individual well-being but also builds trust and cooperation among diverse groups, which is vital in a society facing significant ideological rifts.

To revitalize community involvement, local initiatives must be designed to encourage participation across demographic lines. Schools, local governments, and community organizations can play a pivotal role in creating programs that foster inclusivity and encourage dialogue among residents.

Initiatives such as town hall meetings, community forums, and collaborative projects can provide platforms for citizens to voice their concerns, share their perspectives, and work together on solutions. This grassroots approach not only empowers individuals but also cultivates a culture of civic engagement that can counteract the prevailing narratives of division.

Moreover, leveraging technology can greatly enhance community involvement. Digital platforms that facilitate communication and organization can help bridge gaps between citizens with differing viewpoints. Social media can be harnessed to amplify community events, share local news, and create virtual spaces for discussion.

However, it is crucial to approach this technological integration with a focus on fostering constructive dialogue rather than exacerbating divisions. Educating citizens on digital literacy and critical thinking can empower them to engage more effectively and thoughtfully in online spaces.

Another key aspect of revitalizing community involvement is intergenerational engagement. Programs that connect younger and older generations can enrich community life and promote a deeper understanding of diverse perspectives. Initiatives such as mentorship programs, joint community service projects, and storytelling events can create meaningful connections across age groups.

This engagement not only helps to preserve the rich history of local communities but also ensures that younger citizens are equipped with the knowledge and experience necessary to navigate the complexities of civic life.

Ultimately, revitalizing community involvement is a shared responsibility that requires commitment from individuals, organizations, and institutions alike. By prioritizing inclusive engagement, leveraging technology responsibly, and fostering intergenerational connections, communities can cultivate a robust civic culture.

This culture of participation will not only serve to mitigate polarization but also reinforce the foundational principles of democracy, ensuring that all voices are heard and valued in the ongoing pursuit of a more united and resilient society.

Chapter 7: Paths to Reconciliation

Strategies for Bridging the Divide

Bridging the divide in American society requires a multifaceted approach that acknowledges the complexities of polarization while fostering dialogue and understanding. One effective strategy is promoting open forums and community discussions that bring together individuals from differing political backgrounds. These gatherings can serve as safe spaces for dialogue, encouraging participants to share personal stories and perspectives.

By focusing on human experiences rather than political ideologies, these discussions can help dismantle stereotypes and encourage empathy among individuals who may otherwise view each other as adversaries.

Educational initiatives play a crucial role in bridging the ideological chasm. Implementing programs that teach critical thinking skills and media literacy in schools can empower the younger generation to engage with diverse viewpoints. By equipping citizens with the tools to analyze information critically, they are less likely to fall prey to misinformation and more likely to participate in informed discussions.

Additionally, community-based workshops that emphasize the importance of listening and understanding differing opinions can create a foundation for respectful dialogues across political divides.

Another important strategy involves leveraging technology to foster constructive conversations. Online platforms can facilitate discussions that may not occur in traditional settings, allowing people to connect with those outside their immediate social circles.

However, it is essential to establish guidelines that promote civil discourse and discourage harmful rhetoric.

Social media campaigns that highlight stories of collaboration and mutual understanding can inspire individuals to seek common ground, demonstrating that progress is achievable through collective effort rather than division.

Engaging local leaders and organizations is vital for grassroots movements aimed at bridging divides. Community leaders can act as mediators, facilitating discussions and promoting initiatives that prioritize unity over division. Collaborations among diverse organizations can also amplify efforts to address shared concerns, such as economic inequality or public health crises.

By focusing on issues that resonate across the political spectrum, these alliances can foster a sense of shared purpose, helping to rebuild trust and cooperation among constituents.

Finally, it is essential to cultivate a culture of accountability and responsibility among elected officials and media outlets. Encouraging leaders to prioritize bipartisanship and to model respectful discourse can set a tone that resonates with the electorate. In addition, advocating for responsible journalism that emphasizes balanced reporting can help reduce sensationalism and foster a more informed public.

By creating an environment where respectful dialogue is valued and pursued, the nation can begin to heal the divisions that threaten its democratic foundations, steering away from the specter of conflict and towards a more unified future.

The Role of Education in Fostering Understanding

Education plays a critical role in fostering understanding among citizens, particularly in a democracy characterized by polarization. In the context of the United States, where divergent viewpoints often clash, education serves as a vital tool for promoting informed discourse and civic engagement.

By equipping individuals with the ability to critically analyze information and engage with diverse perspectives, education can help mitigate the divisive tendencies that threaten the fabric of American democracy. This endeavor is not merely about imparting knowledge; it involves cultivating the skills necessary for individuals to navigate complex societal issues and contribute meaningfully to public discourse.

Curricula that prioritize civic education and critical thinking can empower students to appreciate the nuances of political debate and the importance of compromise. Understanding historical contexts, constitutional principles, and the mechanics of governance fosters a sense of civic responsibility and encourages active participation in democratic processes.

As citizens become more educated about their rights and responsibilities, they are better positioned to advocate for their interests while also considering the perspectives of others. This balanced approach is essential in a democracy where the risk of polarization can lead to disengagement or, worse, conflict.

Moreover, education can serve as a bridge across divides by promoting dialogue and collaboration among individuals with differing viewpoints. Programs that encourage community engagement and facilitate discussions on contentious issues can help break down barriers and foster mutual respect. When individuals engage in constructive conversations, they are more likely to find common ground and develop a shared sense of purpose.

This process is crucial in a polarized environment where individuals may be inclined to retreat into echo chambers, reinforcing their biases rather than challenging them.

The role of education extends beyond formal institutions; it encompasses lifelong learning opportunities that can occur in various settings, including community organizations, workplaces, and online platforms. Adult education initiatives that focus on media literacy, conflict resolution, and cultural competency can play a significant role in addressing the challenges posed by misinformation and societal division.

As the electorate becomes more discerning consumers of information, they can better resist the allure of divisive rhetoric and contribute to a more informed and cohesive society.

Ultimately, the future of American democracy hinges on the collective understanding of its citizens. As we navigate an increasingly polarized landscape, prioritizing education that fosters understanding is not merely an option; it is a necessity. By investing in the educational infrastructure that promotes critical thinking, civic engagement, and dialogue, we can cultivate a more resilient democracy capable of withstanding the pressures of division.

In doing so, we take significant strides toward ensuring a future where mutual respect and cooperation prevail over conflict and discord.

Media Literacy and Responsible Consumption

Media literacy is increasingly recognized as a vital component of an informed and engaged electorate, particularly in a polarized political landscape. As the quantity and variety of information sources expand, the challenge of discerning credible information from misinformation becomes more pronounced. This subchapter emphasizes the importance of cultivating media literacy skills among the U.S. electorate.

By equipping citizens with the tools to critically evaluate media content, we can foster a more informed public that is capable of engaging in constructive dialogue and making informed decisions at the ballot box.

The rise of social media platforms has transformed the way information is disseminated and consumed. While these platforms provide opportunities for diverse voices to be heard, they also serve as breeding grounds for misinformation and echo chambers that reinforce existing biases. The tendency to gravitate towards information that aligns with one's preexisting beliefs exacerbates polarization and hampers meaningful discourse.

Thus, it is essential for voters to develop the ability to recognize bias in media, understand the distinction between opinion and fact, and question the sources of their information.

Responsible consumption of media also entails an understanding of the broader impacts of sharing information. In a digital age where content can be rapidly disseminated, individuals must be aware of the consequences of their actions in the information ecosystem. Sharing unverified information can contribute to the spread of false narratives, further entrenching divisions within society.

Promoting a culture of responsibility in media consumption involves encouraging individuals to verify information before sharing it and to engage with a wide range of viewpoints. This practice not only fosters a more informed electorate but also cultivates a sense of communal responsibility in guarding against misinformation.

Educational initiatives play a crucial role in enhancing media literacy among citizens. Schools, community organizations, and even political institutions can implement programs aimed at teaching critical thinking skills and media analysis. By integrating media literacy into curricula and public discourse, we empower individuals to navigate the complexities of modern information landscapes.

Furthermore, collaborations between educational institutions and technology companies can yield resources that facilitate better understanding of how algorithms influence information exposure and the importance of diverse media consumption.

Ultimately, fostering media literacy and responsible consumption is imperative for the health of American democracy. As citizens become more adept at critically engaging with information, they are better positioned to participate in democratic processes meaningfully. This shift not only contributes to a more informed electorate but also helps to bridge the divides that characterize contemporary political discourse.

In an era where the stakes are high and the potential for conflict looms, nurturing a culture of media literacy may well be one of the most effective strategies for safeguarding the future of American democracy.

Chapter 8: Preparing for the Next Election

Voter Mobilization and Participation

Voter mobilization and participation are crucial elements in the health of American democracy, especially in a landscape increasingly characterized by polarization. In recent elections, the divergence in voter turnout rates among different demographic and political groups has highlighted the urgent need for effective mobilization strategies.

The challenge lies not only in encouraging citizens to exercise their right to vote but also in ensuring that their voices are heard in a system that increasingly appears to favor entrenched interests over grassroots engagement. This subchapter will explore the mechanisms of voter mobilization, the barriers to participation, and the roles that various stakeholders can play in fostering an inclusive democratic process.

Historically, voter mobilization efforts have evolved significantly, adapting to the social and political climate of the times. Grassroots organizations, political parties, and social movements have all played pivotal roles in urging citizens to engage with the electoral process. The rise of social media and digital communication has transformed these efforts, enabling campaigns to reach broader audiences with targeted messaging.

However, this new landscape also presents challenges, including misinformation and the potential for deepening divides. Effective voter mobilization must navigate these complexities to build a more informed electorate, one that is motivated not only by party loyalty but also by a genuine commitment to democratic principles.

Barriers to participation remain a significant concern, particularly for marginalized communities who have historically faced systemic obstacles in the voting process. Issues such as voter ID laws, gerrymandering, and limited access to polling places disproportionately affect low-income individuals and people of color. Addressing these barriers requires a concerted effort from both policymakers and civil society.

Legislative reforms aimed at protecting voting rights, combined with grassroots initiatives that educate and empower citizens, are essential to creating a more equitable electoral landscape. Without these efforts, the risk of disenfranchisement could undermine the very foundation of American democracy.

The role of civic education cannot be overstated in the context of voter mobilization. An informed electorate is essential for a functioning democracy, yet there is a growing concern that many citizens lack the knowledge necessary to engage meaningfully in the political process. Educational initiatives that focus on the importance of voting, the mechanics of the electoral system, and the impact of local and national policies can inspire greater participation.

Schools, community organizations, and media outlets must collaborate to create a culture of civic engagement that encourages individuals to take ownership of their democratic rights and responsibilities.

As America navigates its polarized future, the imperative for comprehensive voter mobilization strategies becomes increasingly clear. The potential for a new civil conflict is exacerbated by political disenfranchisement and apathy. To counter this trend, it is essential for all stakeholders—government entities, non-profits, and the electorate itself—to work towards a more inclusive and participatory democracy.

By addressing barriers to participation, enhancing civic education, and leveraging technology for engagement, the United States can foster a political environment that not only encourages voter mobilization but also strengthens the fabric of democracy for generations to come.

The Role of Election Integrity

The role of election integrity in American democracy cannot be overstated, particularly in an era marked by polarization and distrust. Election integrity encompasses the processes and measures that ensure elections are conducted fairly, transparently, and in accordance with the law. It serves as the bedrock of democratic governance, affirming citizens' confidence in electoral outcomes.

In a landscape where accusations of fraud and disenfranchisement abound, safeguarding the integrity of elections is essential for maintaining the legitimacy of democratic institutions and the very fabric of civil society.

A key aspect of election integrity is the implementation of robust security measures that protect against fraud and manipulation. This includes the use of secure voting technologies, stringent verification processes for voter registration, and transparent ballot counting procedures. By ensuring that these systems are resilient against both external and internal threats, election officials can foster a sense of trust among the electorate.

When voters believe that their votes are counted accurately and that the electoral process is safeguarded against interference, they are more likely to engage in the democratic process and accept the outcomes, no matter the results.

Moreover, election integrity is closely linked to the principle of inclusivity within the democratic framework. A truly representative democracy requires that all eligible citizens have the opportunity to participate in elections without undue barriers. This means addressing issues such as gerrymandering, voter ID laws, and access to polling places.

By actively working to dismantle systemic obstacles that disproportionately affect marginalized communities, the electoral system can reflect the diverse voices of the populace. This inclusivity not only strengthens the democratic process but also helps to mitigate feelings of disenfranchisement that can lead to civil unrest.

In the context of America's polarized future, the role of election integrity also extends to the political discourse surrounding elections. Misinformation and disinformation campaigns can undermine public confidence, leading to skepticism about the validity of electoral outcomes. It is imperative for policymakers, civic organizations, and the media to engage in responsible communication about the electoral process.

This involves promoting accurate information about voting procedures, election security measures, and the importance of civic engagement. By fostering an informed electorate, the risks of divisiveness and conflict can be reduced, thus reinforcing the stability of democratic institutions.

Ultimately, the preservation of election integrity is a collective responsibility that requires the active participation of citizens, policymakers, and electoral officials alike. As America grapples with the potential for deepening divisions, reinforcing the integrity of elections can serve as a unifying force. When citizens believe in the legitimacy of the electoral process, they are more likely to engage in constructive dialogue and seek consensus rather than conflict.

In navigating the future of American democracy, prioritizing election integrity will be crucial in preventing the descent into a new civil conflict and ensuring that democracy remains a viable pathway for collective governance.

Addressing Misinformation and Disinformation

Misinformation and disinformation represent significant threats to the integrity of American democracy, particularly in an era characterized by increased polarization. The distinction between the two is crucial: misinformation refers to the unintentional spread of false information, while disinformation involves the deliberate dissemination of falsehoods with the intent to deceive.

Both pose challenges for the electorate, as they can distort public perception, influence voter behavior, and undermine trust in democratic institutions. To address these issues effectively, a multifaceted approach is required that encompasses education, technology, and community engagement.

One of the foundational strategies in combating misinformation is enhancing media literacy among the electorate. By equipping citizens with the critical thinking skills necessary to evaluate information sources, individuals can become more discerning consumers of news. This involves not only understanding the motivations behind various media outlets but also recognizing common tactics used in the spread of false information.

Educational initiatives, whether through formal schooling or community workshops, can empower voters to navigate the complexities of the information landscape, fostering a more informed electorate capable of making sound decisions based on factual evidence.

In addition to education, technology plays a pivotal role in addressing misinformation and disinformation. Social media platforms, which are often breeding grounds for false narratives, must take responsibility for the content shared on their sites. This includes implementing robust fact-checking mechanisms, flagging misleading information, and promoting credible sources.

Collaboration between tech companies, independent fact-checkers, and governmental bodies can create a more transparent information ecosystem that prioritizes accuracy over sensationalism. Moreover, algorithms should be designed to reduce the visibility of false information, thereby limiting its impact on public discourse.

Community engagement is another critical component in the fight against misinformation. Grassroots organizations can foster dialogue among diverse groups, allowing citizens to share their perspectives and challenge misleading narratives in a constructive manner. By creating spaces for open discussion, communities can build resilience against divisive rhetoric and cultivate a sense of shared understanding.

Initiatives aimed at building trust within communities can also mitigate the effects of misinformation, as citizens are more likely to rely on information from trusted local sources.

Ultimately, addressing misinformation and disinformation requires a commitment from all sectors of society, including government, technology, education, and civil society. The stakes are high, as the erosion of trust in democratic processes could lead to a fracturing of societal cohesion.

By taking proactive measures to educate the electorate, leverage technology responsibly, and engage communities in meaningful dialogue, the United States can work toward a more informed and resilient democracy. As the nation grapples with its polarized future, the ability to discern truth from falsehoods will be paramount in ensuring that democracy does not falter in the face of these challenges.

Chapter 9: Imagining a Unified Future

Visioning a Collaborative America

Visioning a Collaborative America requires a profound understanding of the current state of American democracy and the pressing need for unity in the face of polarization. As citizens, we must recognize that our democratic institutions are at a critical juncture. The increasing divide among various factions threatens not only our political landscape but also the very fabric of our society.

By envisioning a collaborative America, we can foster a renewed sense of purpose and inclusivity, allowing diverse voices to coexist and thrive within a shared democratic framework.

Collaboration in a democratic context implies more than mere tolerance; it demands active engagement and mutual respect among individuals with differing viewpoints. For America to move forward, citizens must embrace the idea that differing opinions are not adversaries but rather opportunities for growth and understanding.

This vision calls for a commitment to civil discourse, where debates are grounded in respect and empathy rather than hostility. By prioritizing dialogue, we can dismantle the barriers that have led to mistrust and animosity, paving the way for a more cohesive society.

Moreover, a collaborative America relies on the recognition that local communities play a vital role in shaping our national identity.

Grassroots initiatives can serve as effective platforms for fostering collaboration, where individuals can come together to address pressing issues in their neighborhoods.

By empowering local leaders and encouraging civic participation, we can cultivate a sense of ownership among citizens, reinforcing the notion that democracy is not merely an abstract concept but a lived experience. This localized approach ensures that diverse perspectives are represented, creating solutions that are reflective of the communities they serve.

Educational institutions also have a crucial role in this vision. By promoting curricula that emphasize critical thinking, empathy, and the importance of civic engagement, we can equip future generations with the tools necessary to navigate a polarized landscape. Education should encourage students to explore multiple perspectives and engage in constructive dialogue, fostering a culture where collaboration is valued over division.

This foundational shift can help to cultivate a citizenry that approaches democratic participation with an open mind and a commitment to collective well-being.

In conclusion, envisioning a Collaborative America is not simply an aspirational goal; it is an essential strategy for preserving and enhancing our democracy. As the electorate, we must be proactive in advocating for policies and practices that encourage collaboration and understanding. By embracing our shared humanity and recognizing the power of inclusive dialogue, we can work together to navigate the challenges ahead.

The path to a more unified and resilient democracy lies in our collective hands, and it is through collaboration that we can ensure a brighter future for all Americans.

The Role of Empathy in Politics

Empathy plays a critical role in the landscape of American politics, particularly in an era marked by deep polarization. As citizens engage in political discourse, the ability to understand and share the feelings of others becomes essential for fostering constructive dialogue. In a democracy that thrives on the participation of its electorate, empathy can bridge divides, enabling individuals to connect across ideological lines.

By recognizing the humanity in opposing viewpoints, voters can cultivate a political culture that prioritizes collaboration over conflict.

In recent years, the absence of empathy in political interactions has contributed significantly to the fragmentation of American society. Political leaders and their supporters often resort to dehumanizing language, which further entrenches partisan divides. This lack of understanding not only undermines the democratic process but also fuels animosity among constituents.

When empathy is sidelined, the potential for compromise diminishes, and the likelihood of escalating tensions increases, leaving the nation vulnerable to a deeper schism.

Empathy in politics is not merely an emotional response; it is a strategic imperative for sustaining democracy. Engaging empathetically allows politicians and constituents alike to appreciate the diverse experiences that shape public opinion. By listening actively and valuing differing perspectives, elected officials can craft policies that reflect the needs of a broader constituency.

This approach not only enhances the legitimacy of democratic governance but also encourages civic engagement, as citizens feel seen and heard in the political arena.

Moreover, fostering empathy can mitigate the risks of political violence and social unrest. In a climate where many fear the prospect of a new civil war, understanding and compassion become vital tools for conflict resolution. By investing in empathetic communication, communities can work toward healing and reconciliation, addressing grievances before they escalate into more severe confrontations.

This proactive stance not only preserves democratic ideals but also builds resilience against the divisive forces threatening the nation's stability.

Ultimately, the future of American democracy hinges on the electorate's commitment to embracing empathy as a guiding principle in political engagement. As voters navigate the complexities of a polarized landscape, prioritizing empathy can yield significant dividends. It offers a pathway toward a more inclusive political discourse, fostering a sense of shared purpose and collective responsibility.

In doing so, the electorate can help ensure that democracy not only survives but thrives, steering clear of the precipice of conflict and division.

Building a Resilient Democracy

Building a resilient democracy requires a collective commitment to the principles that underpin a functioning society. As the fabric of American democracy frays, it becomes increasingly vital to engage citizens in a dialogue about the core values of freedom, justice, and equality. This engagement must extend beyond the ballot box, fostering a culture of active participation where citizens are not only voters but also informed advocates for their communities.

A resilient democracy thrives when individuals understand their rights and responsibilities, actively participating in civic life to hold leaders accountable and ensure that government reflects the will of the people.

Education plays a pivotal role in cultivating a resilient democracy. An informed electorate is essential for making sound decisions that impact governance and societal well-being. Schools and community organizations must prioritize civic education, equipping individuals with the knowledge necessary to navigate complex political landscapes. This education should emphasize critical thinking, media literacy, and the importance of diverse perspectives.

By fostering an environment where individuals can engage with differing viewpoints, society can mitigate the polarization that currently undermines democratic discourse.

Furthermore, building a resilient democracy necessitates the reinforcement of institutions that uphold the rule of law and protect individual rights. This includes ensuring the independence of the judiciary, promoting transparency in government, and safeguarding the rights of assembly and free speech.

When institutions are perceived as fair and just, public trust is cultivated, and citizens are more likely to engage in the political process. Strengthening these institutions also involves addressing systemic inequalities that can disenfranchise marginalized communities, ensuring that every voice is heard and represented in the democratic process.

Community engagement and grassroots movements are essential components of a resilient democracy. By mobilizing citizens at the local level, communities can address specific challenges and advocate for policies that reflect their needs and values. Grassroots efforts can bridge divides, fostering collaboration among diverse groups and creating a sense of shared purpose.

These movements not only empower individuals but also serve as a counterbalance to entrenched interests that may seek to undermine democratic principles. Encouraging civic participation through local initiatives can reinvigorate the democratic process and build a more cohesive society.

Finally, the future of American democracy hinges on the ability to address polarization through dialogue and compromise. A resilient democracy must be capable of adapting to change while remaining committed to its foundational principles. This involves recognizing the legitimate grievances of various groups and finding common ground to foster collaboration rather than conflict.

Embracing a culture of dialogue, where differences are acknowledged and respected, can help to heal divisions and reinforce the idea that democracy is a shared endeavor. In navigating America's polarized future, the electorate must prioritize unity and resilience, ensuring that democracy not only survives but thrives.

Chapter 10: Conclusion: The Call to Action

Reflecting on the Stakes of Democracy

The stakes of democracy in America are at a critical juncture, as the nation grapples with increasing polarization that threatens the very fabric of its democratic institutions. The historical context of American democracy illustrates a system designed to adapt and endure through challenges. However, the current climate, marked by deep ideological divides, raises questions about the resilience of these institutions.

As citizens, understanding the implications of this polarization is essential to safeguarding democracy and ensuring that it serves the collective interests of the populace rather than fragmenting into opposing factions.

The disintegration of civil discourse has profound implications for democratic engagement. When citizens retreat into echo chambers, where their beliefs are constantly reinforced and opposing views are vilified, the foundation of democracy erodes. This polarization not only stifles meaningful dialogue but also fosters an environment where misinformation thrives.

As the electorate navigates this complex landscape, it becomes imperative to prioritize the pursuit of common ground and mutual understanding. By fostering a culture of dialogue and critical thinking, Americans can reclaim the narrative and ensure that democracy remains a space for diverse perspectives.

The question of whether America is facing a new civil war is not merely rhetorical; it is a pressing concern that demands careful examination. The rise of political violence and the normalization of extreme rhetoric signal a dangerous trend that echoes past conflicts. Policymakers, community leaders, and citizens must recognize that the stakes are not limited to political victories or losses, but encompass the very essence of national unity and social cohesion.

A commitment to democratic principles necessitates a collective effort to address the underlying grievances that fuel division and animosity.

Moreover, the role of institutions in preserving democracy cannot be overstated. Strong, independent institutions serve as a bulwark against authoritarian tendencies and provide mechanisms for accountability. The judiciary, the press, and civic organizations play crucial roles in fostering transparency and upholding the rule of law.

As the electorate considers the future of American democracy, it is vital to advocate for and protect these institutions from erosion. Strengthening institutional integrity is essential for restoring public trust and ensuring that democracy functions effectively for all citizens.

Ultimately, reflecting on the stakes of democracy requires a commitment to active participation and responsible citizenship. Each individual bears the responsibility to engage thoughtfully in the political process, recognizing that apathy and disengagement only exacerbate the challenges facing democracy. As the electorate contemplates the future, it is crucial to embrace the values of tolerance, empathy, and civic responsibility.

By doing so, Americans can navigate the polarized landscape and work towards a more inclusive and resilient democratic society.

Encouraging Active Citizenship

Encouraging active citizenship is essential for fostering a robust democracy, particularly in an era marked by polarization and division. Active citizenship goes beyond mere participation in elections; it encompasses engagement in community initiatives, public discussions, and civic organizations.

By promoting a culture of active citizenship, we can strengthen the social fabric of our communities and ensure that diverse voices and perspectives are included in the democratic process. This engagement is crucial in countering the apathy that often accompanies political disillusionment, which can lead to further polarization and a potential erosion of democratic norms.

Education plays a pivotal role in cultivating active citizenship. By equipping citizens with the knowledge of their rights and responsibilities, as well as an understanding of the political system, we empower individuals to take an informed stance on issues that matter to them. Educational institutions can serve as incubators for civic engagement, encouraging students to participate in debates, volunteer for local initiatives, and engage with their representatives.

This foundation not only prepares the next generation for leadership roles but also fosters a sense of ownership over the democratic process, encouraging individuals to advocate for their communities.

Moreover, fostering active citizenship requires creating spaces for dialogue and collaboration among diverse groups. Community forums, town hall meetings, and online platforms can serve as venues for individuals to express their opinions, share experiences, and work collaboratively toward common goals. These interactions help to bridge divides by humanizing differing viewpoints and promoting empathy.

When citizens engage in constructive conversations, they are more likely to find common ground, which can diminish the likelihood of conflict and promote a more cohesive society.

In addition to dialogue, supporting grassroots movements and local organizations is vital for encouraging active citizenship. These entities often address specific community needs and empower individuals to take action. By providing resources and support to local initiatives, we can amplify the voices of those who may feel marginalized or overlooked in broader political discussions.

This grassroots engagement not only addresses immediate concerns but also nurtures a generation of leaders who are committed to public service and civic responsibility.

Ultimately, encouraging active citizenship is a collective effort that requires commitment from individuals, institutions, and policymakers alike. By prioritizing civic engagement and fostering environments where diverse voices are heard, we can counteract the forces of division that threaten our democracy.

As we navigate the complexities of our polarized future, it is imperative that we recognize the power of active citizenship in shaping a more inclusive and resilient democratic society. The future of American democracy hinges on our ability to inspire and mobilize citizens to become active participants in the democratic process, ensuring that it remains vibrant and responsive to the needs of all.

The Path Forward: Hope Amidst Challenges

The future of American democracy hangs in a delicate balance, influenced by deep-seated divisions that threaten to fracture the nation. Yet, amidst the challenges that loom large, there exists a palpable sense of hope. Citizens are increasingly aware of the need for constructive dialogue and collaboration across ideological divides. This awakening presents an opportunity for the electorate to reclaim the democratic principles that have historically united the country.

Engaging in open conversations about shared values can lay the groundwork for a more resilient democracy, one where differences are acknowledged but not weaponized.

Grassroots movements are emerging as powerful catalysts for change, driven by citizens who refuse to be passive observers in the democratic process. These movements are not only advocating for policy reforms but also promoting a culture of empathy and understanding. By prioritizing community engagement and fostering local initiatives, individuals are taking action to bridge divides and rebuild trust in democratic institutions.

This grassroots approach empowers citizens to have a tangible impact on their governance, illustrating that democracy is not solely the responsibility of elected officials but a collective endeavor.

Education plays a critical role in shaping the future of American democracy. By enhancing civic education and promoting critical thinking skills, the electorate can cultivate a more informed citizenry capable of engaging in thoughtful discourse. Educational initiatives that emphasize the importance of diverse perspectives can help dismantle the echo chambers that contribute to polarization.

As citizens become more informed about the complexities of governance and policy, they are better equipped to participate in democratic processes, advocate for their interests, and hold leaders accountable.

The role of technology in fostering a more connected and informed electorate cannot be overlooked. While social media has been a double-edged sword, it also offers platforms for dialogue and mobilization. By harnessing technology to facilitate constructive conversations and promote civic engagement, Americans can transcend geographical and ideological barriers.

Initiatives that encourage respectful online discourse can help mitigate the toxic environment that often characterizes political discussions, fostering a culture of collaboration and mutual respect.

Ultimately, the path forward for American democracy requires a commitment from all citizens to actively participate in the political process. This involves not only voting but also engaging in community dialogues, advocating for reforms, and supporting candidates who prioritize unity over division.

Hope exists in the collective resolve of the electorate to confront the challenges ahead, recognizing that a thriving democracy is built on the principles of inclusivity, compromise, and shared responsibility. By embracing these ideals, Americans can work together to navigate the tumultuous landscape and chart a course towards a more unified and democratic future.